Secrets of Dark Psychology and Manipulation in 2020

Discover the Secret techniques used in Dark Psychology that manipulators use to take control of their victims, through NLP, Suggestions, Persuasion and Influence.

By

Nick Reynolds

Disclaimer Notice

Table of Contents

Chapter 1:

What is Dark Psychology

Everyone at some point or another uses dark psychology to manipulate and influence someone to get what they want or get them to take a specific type of action. Dark Psychology is when some use psychological tactics to manipulate and influence others to action. The psychological tactics the manipulator will use include motivation, persuasion, emotion, and coercion to achieve what they want.

Manipulators use Dark Psychology to prey upon others, victimize them, bully them to get what they want them to do. I will provide information in this book, which will allow you to identify, pick up when a manipulator is using dark psychological tactics on you to accomplish their desired purpose. We will examine the different ways manipulators use dark psychology to influence people and how you can identify them to protect yourself from manipulation.

Machivalism

Niccolo Machiavelli

Niccolo Machiavelli was born on May 3, 1469, in Italy, after 14 years of being a diplomat in his country, he was exiled during the Medici family exile. When the Medici family regained power, he was jailed for some time. During which he wrote the infamous book The Prince, which explains how to deal with political affairs in a self-serving and ruthless manner. He also followed up with that book release by writing a lot more books leading up to his death on June 21, 1527.

Niccolo believed that if rulers were to maintain their reign and possess the power they cannot do so through good deeds and peaceful reign. It's generally thought that rulers that do good and are favored by the people are often the ones that will outlast the opposition. However, Niccolo disagreed with conventional standards. Instead, Niccolo believed that one has to hold power through force and ruthlessness, he believed that being good will ensure no power and no one will maintain virtue through being good alone.

Machiavelli believed that all rulers and commanders' only concern and sole purpose should be to acquire power. Machiavelli argues that legitimate rulership is when an individual has actual possession of power, he argues that good and are not sufficient to win and maintain control of anything.

Machiavelli believes that once individuals know how to use the proper application of power that's when people will begin to obey the ruler.

Machiavellianism is a trait where people will try to manipulate their interpersonal relationships, through having no emotional attachment, only coercion by force. The trait was named off of political psychologist

Niccolo Machiavelli himself. Machiavellianism is a formed human behavior that can be noticed a lot among narcissists. Machiavelli believes that treachery and deceit would be more expedient than honesty and virtue.

Machiavelli believes that force and emotional coldness is more effective when people are in positions of leadership, even if that is not their natural personality type trait.

In Machiavellism, you have "High Machs" and "Low Machs", the personality type that is naturally a Machiavellian is considered "High Machs" which are master manipulators that naturally use treachery and are forced to have their way. While others that merely choose or adapt the philosophy are considered to be "Low Machs". High Machs don't need to acquire the skills to manipulate people, they are already naturally conniving and deceptive. They will use other people as stepping stones to get what they want and achieve their objectives. Machiavellians, don't feel guilty or empathize with others when it comes to them accomplishing what they set out to accomplish. In their mind, they believe that it's better you than them, they should control you than you control them. Machiavellianism is a part of what's considered as the "Dark Triad", the other two personality traits included are psychopaths and narcissists. They all have poor emotional intelligence, lacking in empathy and honesty.

Machiavellians are very strategic in how they operate, they are willing to lie, cheat, and deceive anyone even their families. Because of their lack of emotional attachment they can be a danger to other people, they will not hold back if it is that they need to harm others to achieve their goals. Unlike the other personality traits that are a part of the Dark Triad, that may arm others for enjoyment or lack of empathy. Machiavellians are only interested in manipulating and deceiving others to gain power. Even though Machiavellians may not express empathy towards people, they do have the ability to understand the emotions and feelings of others and don't care much about them. Machiavellianism will see you suffering, or hurting and do not care much about you to change their actions. Some evolutionary psychologists consider Machiavellians to be advantageous, because of their ability to go after their goals, with little much thought or consideration for others. Because of this, Machiavellians find it hard to develop long-lasting relationships with others, because they find it challenging to resonate with people that do not see their way of operating.

Machiavellians are considered as being alexithymia, which is a deficit in identifying and understanding one's emotions. People that are alexithymia are cold, and out of touch with their emotions.

Alexithymia is a personality disorder where people are unable to give meaning to their emotions. They are emotionally detached and lack awareness and social attachment to other people. People who experience alexithymia have issues with recognizing other people's emotions. This is considered a disorder, when they experience the inability to verbalize their emotions, they find it hard to remember their dreams, fantasize about life, and react to others' emotions. They find it very difficult to show empathy towards others, even though Machiavellism embodied some of these characteristics in their approach to dealing with people. The difference is that machiavellist do feel the emotions of others at times, but they detach themselves from the emotions so that they can make the tough decisions to gain or maintain power.

Low Machs

Low Machs are more emotionally in touch, they are more empathetic towards people, they can relate to others in a way that high Machs can't. They are not natural machs, they are the type that developed the trait over time either as a skill or as a result of significant life events. Low Machs are more submissive, they are good people that others like to be around, they are considerate and believe that people sometimes must be given a second chance. They have no problem accepting direction imposed on them, they are not that motivated by being in a position of power or status. They like to win, but if they lose they accept it as a part of life, unlike the high machs that will do anything necessary to win or have their way. They operate with more ethical standards than their counterparts. Low Machs know how to make use of their Machiavellianism with its time to, and when to take it easy and be considerate of others.

They are the perfect machs for managerial roles, they can command just enough respect from their colleagues without being disliked because of their harsh behaviors.

High Machs

High Machs are focused on themselves and their well being, they believe that they have to be deceptive and ruthless to get ahead in life. They don't trust people easily and believe that relying on people's goodness is naive and can do you more harm than good. They prioritize the power of love and connection. People who are high machs are extremely goal-oriented and will do anything necessary for them to achieve their goals. Even if it means that they have to engage in unethical behaviors. People who are High Machs have a natural Machiavelli personality trait, they have almost no empathy and are emotionally detached. They are the master manipulators, they will use all anything available to achieve their ends. 'People with high Mach personality have been found to engage in counterproductive behaviors such as lying, theft, bullying, and numerous others' (Belchad.F, 2018).

Machiavelli believes that it's best to tell people what they want to hear, you will often see them flattering important people to get them to lower their guard or gain their trust. They function best when the rules are ambiguous where they can have their ways, and take control of a situation or the room. They will use tactics such as charm, friendliness, and flattery to get over at people. The high machs prefer to be subtle and mask their true intentions so that they can protect themselves from being detected. And once they have control or some level of power they will begin to use pressure, threats, and aggressive coercion to get what they want.

Machiavellianism Inside the Organisation

Employees in the organization that display high machs tendencies are predisposed to engage in unethical behavior inside the organization. Because they are driven to do whatever they need to do to accomplish their goals and objectives. Which can also be used as a positive inside the organization once they are steered in the correct direction. Even though Machiavellians are uncommon in the organization, some of the employees in the organization lean closer to high machs, and some lean close to low machs. Employees with high machs inside the organization will tend to hide information or how-to skills, they do not have the type of helping behavior that's often required. They will limit the spread of information so that they can maintain some level of power and control. So when high machs are under low machs leadership, they tend to not respond well under those types of conditions.

High Machs can contribute to the unethical nature of the organization if they can flourish they can turn the organization to an unethical one. Most people, employers try to avoid high machs inside the organization. High Mach individuals are very proficient in unethical and manipulating environments. Some have noted that high machs can also do well and show pro-organizational behavior if they see where it is beneficial to them when it comes to achieving their goals. Every organization has them, maybe even most organizations with a decent number of employees, the trick to working with high machs is to understand who they are and how they think and operate. The better you understand them, the more success you will have with managing the relationship.

Machiavellianism is identified as a quantitative trait, which means that some people are more prone to display that trait more than others. Machiavellianism is willing to go to any lengths to achieve their goals, they are extremely focused and only care about achievements and winning. Because of this they are very resourceful and will use any means necessary to accomplish their goals, even if it means that they need to bend the rules or manipulate others. High machs have a cynical worldview, which contributes to them always expecting the worst from other people that they deal with. This justifies them to do as they do, and act how they act, they find it hard to trust their peers and believe that people are always out to get them. The thing with High Machs is that they won't just randomly go around and make trouble, they will only engage in a situation if it's benefiting them.

They will go all the way, engage in sabotage, manipulate people or even hurt others to meet their ends.

Chapter 2:

The Narcissist

Narcissists have a pattern of being grandiose, having an overwhelming need for admiration and praise, but express very little empathy towards others. They can act snobbish, rude, and very disrespectful towards other people. Narcissism is a type of personality disorder where people have an inflated sense of their ego, they think of and only hire themselves and have a lack of empathy towards others. Because narcissists mostly think about themselves and have a disregard for others, this type of attitude usually causes a lot of problems when it comes to relationships, whether it be professional, friendship, or intimate. Because of how they think and their egos, it causes other people to not want to be around them.

Narcissists believe in themselves that they have to be the best in anything and everything that they do no matter what the circumstances. They believe they are always the most competent for the job and when they are in the job, they must be in a position of control, feeling superior to everyone else. Even though they are selfish and behave as if they need no one to help them reach their highest potential, they still have a need to constantly seek attention. They like to do things that will constantly attract attention from people, they will do anything to constantly seek validation from others. No amount of flattering and admiration is enough for them, they never feel that these things can never be enough. They believe that they will never measure up and are insecure in themselves in a weird kind of way, to put it this way, their insecurities are driven by the fact that they see others ahead of them and they have to constantly measure up, even when they are ahead.

Narcissists are people who are extremely full of themselves and obsessed, this is not to be misunderstood with self-love. They are infatuated with a grandiose image of themselves, they inflate the imagery of themselves in their minds to avoid feeling a sense of insecurity or inferiority. This is what contributes to their dysfunctional attitudes and behavior. People often describe them as cocky, manipulative, and selfish. These types of behavior often spill over into their other relationships. They live inside their egos, so any slight criticism or disagreement from others will offend them and they will see that as a personal attack. Most people that deal with a narcissist on a day to day basis, learn to just accept their demands and go with the flow to avoid any sort of confrontation.

Narcissists believe they are special and unique; they believe that they are God's gift to mankind. They believe they are too good for the average people, and they only want to be around people of high-status, and influence. Because they like people to think highly of them, they will even lie about their achievements and things that they have done, to make themselves seem more accomplished than they are. They require constant praise and admiration from people, they need people to constantly stroke their ego, hence you will see them surrounding themselves with others that will feed them what they want to hear.

Because of their inflated ego, they have this false sense of entitlement, they believe that whatever it is that they want they should have, they believe that people around them should do whatever it is that's necessary to make them get what they want.

Psychopathy

Psychopathy is a personality disorder whereby people that suffer from this disorder often show traits of antisocial behaviors, impaired empathy, remorse, and egotistical behavior. They display similar and overlapping behaviors with sociopaths, but they also have strong differences, which contradict each other.

A sociopath has to do with a person's antisocial tendencies based on social and environmental factors, while psychopaths traits are said to be more innate. Psychopathy in the simpler form can be characterized as the absence of empathy towards other people. Psychopaths have a level of callousness and emotional detachment that will enable them to manipulate other people.

Even though they are so blunt in their behavior they are very hard to identify and pick out.

They can appear to be normal to people, they can even be charming, funny, and charismatic. They will behave in such a way to hide their true intentions especially the ones that will participate in criminal activity.

Psychopaths also have deep desires to be loved and cared for by others, they have a wish to be loved by other people, this desire is oftentimes unfulfilled because of their personality. This leaves them feeling empty and isolated, lacking social networks and interactions. The lives of most psychopaths are absent from social interaction, they can appear as a loner.

Psychopaths feel they are prisoners of their mind, even though they appear to be arrogant, they do feel a sense of inferiority towards their peer group.

Because of their nature, they will try their hardest to hide their true intentions from other people, to fit in.

They will observe others going out and having fun and feel that they will never be a part of that. Psychopaths tend to be sensation seekers always requiring excessive stimulation for adventure and thrill, which can contribute to some level of weakness from them. Psychopaths are often seen to be violent, having a lack of stability in their lives and relationships, having a lack of empathy towards other people, being very impulsive and thrill-seeking, and deceitful. Most of these traits are developed and can be seen from an early age. This personality disorder is considered as lifelong in some people, psychopaths generally have to go through therapy to manage the disorder or they will turn out to be a threat to society. If their personality is detected early and they go through therapy, they can learn how to manage and decrease their tendencies over time.

Chapter 3:

Persuasion

An Experienced manipulator will use persuasion as a means of getting others to do what they want, most times unsuspecting victims have no idea that they are being manipulated. Women and men do this all the time, they will tell you and give you everything you wish so that you can give them what they want or do what they want in return. People that suspect that they are being manipulated can counter the manipulator and protect themselves.

Persuasion is when people try to say or present an argument to motivate others to accomplish their desired results. An individual will do this through using their charisma, or appeal towards your sensing. Persuasion has a way of being direct and indirect, explicit, and implicit. Persuasion will come across more as passive and subtle because very rarely does the perpetrator want anyone to know that they are trying to manipulate each.

The manipulators get people to do what they want through finding the stimulus that will encourage people to take action, the motivation they need to make a change. The history of persuasion began with the Greeks who believed that strong rhetoric and elocution is necessary for a successful politician. As most of their trials were held in front of an assembly and the outcome of the case would be based on the persuasiveness of the speaker, and rhetoric was important to have persuasion in any stance you decided to take.

The types of persuasion people use varies, manipulators often try different ways to convince people that they are telling the truth or get their victims to do what they want them to do.

Manipulators use different types of persuasive techniques depending on the situation, circumstances, and people that they are interacting with.

For some people they require a little bit more convincing than others, so a simple conversation and handshake agreement won't work to win them over.

The Two Modes of Persuasion

There are three modes of persuasion, however only two are relevant to a manipulator, that's the Logos and Pathos. The ethos which is the third mode has to do with an author or writer building credibility through their work, such as a professor, scientist, researcher, etc.

Logos is a type of persuasion that manipulators use; this is when people will use their power and authority to influence or motivate someone to change.

This type of persuasion is used to appeal to reason, manipulators will try to use logic and scientific reasoning to convince people as they desire. This type of persuasion is used during arguments and debates that require proof and evidence to support the idea.

Another type of persuasion technique people use is called pathos, this is when the manipulator tries to motivate action by appealing to emotions. Pathos is not based on proof but rather on how the person feels at the moment. This is a very effective technique to persuade people because most people are ruled by their emotions and their minds. When people try to appeal to your emotions, they will try to appeal to your feelings and imagination. They will try to use excitement, make you feel sad, make you pity them just to get what they want. When you identify situations like this just be aware that the person may be trying to manipulate you.

Chapter 4:

Traits of a Manipulator

Manipulative people tend to have a few consistent traits if you take the time to notice you will see them showing these traits time and again. Can you think if you have ever been in a situation where you were with someone and every time that something bad happens they behaved as if they are the victim? They never think of taking responsibility for their actions, they are quick to blame others and behave as if they are being attacked and victimized. These types of behaviors are signs that the individual may be manipulative.

Manipulators have difficulties with accepting that they have also contributed to the problem, they never accept responsibility for anything that they do.

Instead, they like to blame others and behave as if something happened to them. This is an evident sign that the person is playing a victim role, even though they may not say it directly, they will demonstrate the victim's behaviors in their actions. Manipulative people can do this well, they will even over exaggerate and make up stories about what happened to gain sympathy from others.

Think about the times when you were in a situation where you know the person was wrong, however they somehow turned the situation around to make it seem as if they are innocent. Or they behaved as if they could not control the outcome or that you were the one that hurt them. They will even distort the truth to make it seem like they are being victimized to hide their true intentions and manipulate people to believe what they want them to believe. When you ask them why it is that something happened, they will make excuses, exaggerate the truth, or just simply tell lies.

When manipulators are being questioned they will omit or hide significant information to not be exposed. They know if they say the wrong thing they will be revealed, which is one of the reasons why they stay silent or avoid interrogation. They will be vague as possible when being asked direct questions because they never want what they said to be used against them.

Manipulative people provide what we consider to be 'alternative facts' they will tell untruths, which are not clear lies but they are also not the clear truths.

Manipulators will look for facts and evidence that support their idea while avoiding all the facts which clearly shows that their claims are untrue. What you focus on will be your truth, and your mind will find all the past and present evidence to support your idea.

Manipulative people can be very passive-aggressive, they use this type of behavior to ease themselves out of difficult situations.

Especially when they do not want to be responsible. Have you ever experienced telling someone to do something that you know that they didn't want to do and each time you remind them of it they said that they forgot? That's them being passive-aggressive in their attempt to manipulate the situation. To the simpleton, this may seem as negligence however it's a form of anger that is often unhealthy. They will even refuse to answer your questions, ignoring you as if they did not hear a word you say.

I am sure all of us have experienced when you and another person have some form of disagreement. It could be at work, or even at school and they will walk past you as if you don't even exist. Which often leaves you confused because you are wondering if it's an accident, if they made a mistake, because of how subtle it appears. They won't show that they are angry with you or either allow anyone else to discover their feelings at the moment.

When they do this it's often to get your attention to tell you that something is wrong, that they are not all on good terms with you. It's all an act of manipulation to make you think of them more or get you to say something to them.

A passive-aggressive person will not blatantly refuse your order, but will rather display behavior which suggests that they are not in agreement with what you asked of them. You will see them shaking their heads, sighing or resting their hands on their heads looking distressful. They do value cooperating with others and being a good sport, but deep down inside them they would much rather otherwise. Instead of saying no, they will murmur and complain to others around the outside of your presence. Instead of refusing your request, they will talk about what they have already done for you, and how much they have already contributed and why it is that you keep asking them to do these tasks. Passive-aggressive people will disguise their insults, they will compliment you on something and then use a clause such as 'but'. You will hear them say, "I like you but" "I think you will do well but", "Not to be judging but". They do this to hide or mask their actual aggression or direct insult because they don't want to be perceived as a bad person.

Manipulative people will make you feel guilty about something that happened, they will make you go on a guilt trip. Guilt trips are a form of the manipulative technique used by people that aim to abuse and control you. These types of people are very calculative, they will use guilt as a weapon anything they want from other people.

How they make you feel guilty is by blaming you for things that you have no control over. If they know that you have a soft spot they will use that against you to put you through a guilt trip and manipulate you. The manipulator aims to target your vulnerability and your emotional weaknesses, once they can tap into that, they will wield that sword to cut you in pieces, or coerce you into doing what they want.

The manipulator expects people to come to their rescue all the time, and when you can't they will do anything in their power to force you to.

Manipulative people will never take the blame for any of their faults, they will pretend that the reason everything happens was the cause of someone else. Because of this level of thinking they are very reluctant in helping others resolve the issue that is present. They want to shy away from responsibilities and leave it on others, this is the reason why they often lie or try to justify their negligent behavior, they will perform all sorts of tricks and tactics to untangle themselves out of a situation.

They always have an answer for everything they do, they have all the perfect excuses to justify and rationalize their behavior. They will do this to not be discovered or not be found out. That's how they can maintain their image while they manipulate other people. Manipulators will try to rationalize everything they do, to mislead people, and hide the true nature of their manipulative character.

Rationalizing is a tactic that they use, to get over others, and resist taking responsibility for anything they do. When you are communicating with a manipulator, once they begin to rationalize their thoughts you can instantly tell that something is wrong. If they keep apologizing for an action that they keep repeating, it's a clear sign that they are trying to manipulate you and they are likely to repeat their behavior in the future. Even though they will recognize that they have a problem, they will not change, they will try to appeal to your emotions to make you pity them rather than them changing their ways.

Psychological Coercion

Coercion is an aggressive form of manipulation where one person will try to compel another party to behave in a certain way or perform a specific action through the application of force.

The victimizer will use threat, pressure, intimidation, or any kind of force that will cause their victim to give in. A skilled manipulator will use psychological techniques to coerce or influence specific behavior from their victim. In this case, the victim may feel different emotions such as stress, anxiety, and fear during the psychological coercion.

When a victim is being coerced usually being influenced to perform actionable steps that lead him/her down to an end goal. These steps are sometimes so small they go unnoticed by the victim until later on down the line. Coercion is best done indirectly through the victim's allies and friends so that it goes undetected. That way the victim will not be able to put up their defense as they normally would.

When a person is coerced psychologically this is meant to disarm or overcome their ability to think critically and use their better judgment.

Once the victim's guard is lowered, their cognitive processes and decision-making skills are no longer rational and free-willed.

During psychological coercion the victim will often be threatened in different areas of their lives, such as their relationship with others, they will even be blackmailed (which is also another form of manipulation). The threats can take the form of the risk of exposure to damaging information. Psychological coercion was used by government officials in the past to get people to carry out actions that they were reluctant to do or did not want to perform at all. Such as a confession or resignation.

Victims were coerced and told that if they did not conform they would be exposed and run the risk of public humiliation. Because the victims wanted to protect their families and their reputation, they would go ahead and follow through with the victimizer's requests.

BlackMail

Blackmail is a form of coercion as well, where the perpetrator will use the threat of revealing or exposing its victim to coerce them into doing what they want. Oftentimes the information that can be revealed is damaging to the victims' character and can ruin their reputation for good. In most countries blackmail is illegal and is also considered as a form of extortion, the perpetrator will oftentimes require some form of payment or incentives to not reveal the information of the victim.

In many countries, blackmail is a sanctionable offense that brings a criminal charge. The common type of blackmail that manipulators use is emotional blackmail.

Emotional blackmail usually involves two people that have established some form of close connection which may include friendship, intimate, or family relationships. People that are emotional blackmailers use fear and guilt in their relationships, making others feel fearful of going against them.

The blackmailers make the victim fear to lose what they have or fearful of being separated from a relationship which they deeply cherished or need for security. Especially in a case where the victim is insecure or dependent on the other for their daily living.

Emotional blackmail can cause psychological abuse and permanent damage to the victim mentally and emotionally. Because of the demand of the blackmailer and the risk of exposure the act of blackmail often goes unnoticed and undetected. That's how manipulators get away with their actions and the blackmail can go on for even years. The information the manipulator gains about the victim is used as leverage to drive fear and control over their victims.

We can be emotionally blackmailed by those who love us; it's the ones that are closest to us that often use emotional blackmail. They will use our secrets, and weaknesses to manipulate us and get what they want from us.

Emotional blackmail can show its head in professional relationships, but more often it's through friendships, intimate and family relationships that often expose us to emotional blackmail. Many times we use emotional blackmail in our relationships. But our intentions are light and most times we are not even aware that we are doing it.

Emotional Blackmailers use three strategies over their victims; which are obligation, fear, and guilt. Blackmailers will tap into the victims' minds to make them feel obligated to do something for them to reciprocate a favor. The victim becomes fearful that they must do something, or guilty that they should do something. They will use the secretive information that they have acquired over the years to use against the victim.

Chapter 5:

Manipulation in Relationships

Oftentimes when we are in relationships, intimate relationships we become an emotional wreck, going through emotional roller coasters.

Because we are so wrapped up in the other person and our longing for feeling accepted by the other person, our decisions often become clouded. In a relationship, the manipulator will manipulate the victim by making them feel a sense of guilt through their actions or inactions. What manipulators will do is try to convince you to feel bad for your actions to the point you will begin to admit that you are guilty and do as they desire.

They will make you believe that they are correct and you are wrong, they will make you believe that your actions reflect the way you feel about them whether you love them or not.

Manipulators in relationships will force their insecurities on you to control how you behave towards them. This is powerful because we are emotional creatures and we are driven by emotions and how we feel. They will project their insecurities on you to make you do as they wish, they will even make up lies to make you believe them, and in turn, make you feel guilty about what you want to do.

An example of this is when a partner says that they do not want you to have any friends because their previous relationship was ruined by a friend.

Because there is a fine line between truth and lies, you will have a hard time identifying whether they are genuine or not if you are not aware of what they are doing, it will be misconstrued as actual truth.

Because of all this emotional connection that you have with them, it's easy for them to brainwash you against your personal belief. They will use your insecurities against you to make you doubt yourself. If you have a dream to maybe let's say travel the world and start a new career because they are insecure and have self-doubt they will project that on you and try to dissuade you from going after your dream. They will start to point out your shortcomings, drawbacks, and insecurities to make you doubt your capabilities.

By the time they are through with you, we will have no further desires to make the move or chase any dreams. Often they don't do it with your best interest in mind, neither do they have theirs.

Manipulators only think of themselves and what they want, if they can gain control over you, they will try to control everything you do.

They also have a strange way of making you believe what they want you to believe about yourself and your surroundings. Have you ever noticed that sometimes you will meet a strong intelligent female or male, and then afterward they meet someone and start to behave differently from that point on? You can hardly recognize them for who they once were, that's because they are being manipulated emotionally to the point where they have reshaped their entire identity and who they believe themselves to be. People may think it's natural for someone to adopt the traits and behavior of others, yes but not when they have negative outcomes.

When someone that's normally polite, nice, and has a positive outlook on life meets someone, then their behavior changes and becomes negative. It is usually a sign that something is happening that's not normal. This is usually an indication that they are being manipulated by someone, or you are being manipulated by someone. If you come to realize that your partner's needs are constantly being met more often than yours, this may be a sign that you are being manipulated. This could also be out of genuine love, but if you are doing it out of guilt, or you are feeling guilty when doing it this is possibly a sign of manipulation. Once you have identified that you are being emotionally blackmailed you need to stand your ground and set your boundaries. Ensure that when you are around the manipulator you express your feelings and make sure you hold your ground. If they try to brush your opinion to the side make sure that you reinforce the fact that you are a human which means you have the same amount of rights and deserve the same amount of respect as anyone else.

You need to express to them that your opinions are just as important as theirs, that disagreeing and saying no does not mean that you have anything against them. You need to implement these measures without feeling guilt without feeling as if you are doing something wrong. What the manipulator does is violate your boundaries until they are no more, so they are free to do anything they want, this is the first step to controlling you through manipulation. Where there are no boundaries and no imposed limits means that they are free to do anything they want to do. So it's very important to set boundaries and ensure that others respect them if they want to maintain the relationship they have with you. The sooner you have identified that someone is trying to manipulate you, the better, at that point you will be able to make logical decisions instead of emotional ones that can move you forward. Dealing with a manipulator will have you experiencing the extremes of every emotional experience, at one point you will be very happy, at another point you will be extremely sad. It's the same way how manipulators act and have different faces in front of different people. They do that to hide their deceit and intent to prevent them from being exposed.

Manipulators will never admit their faults and weaknesses, they will always blame other people but themselves for their shortcomings. They do this because they always want you to feel disempowered so that you can surrender to what they want and desire. They will insist on violating your boundaries all the time, then make you feel as if you were the one that caused it. When you feel like you are being manipulated it's very important to stand your ground and assert consequences that will teach the manipulator what is acceptable and not acceptable.

This will compel them to shift the way they treat you and respect the boundaries that you set for yourself.

Hypnotism

Hypnosis is a trance-like state, that a person gets in through relaxation, suggestibility, and heightened imagination. During this state the subject is awake and alert, it's a trance-like state that can be compared to when someone is daydreaming or having a feeling similar to when they are deep inside a great movie. Inside this imaginary world, everything seems real as if you are sleeping and dreaming, it's hard to separate what's fake from what's not real.

During hypnosis, your emotions and senses are fully engaged; this can cause extreme fear, sadness, or happiness. Manipulators can make you go into this state through several different techniques most times you may not even be aware that you were hypnotized until later. You may think this is far fetched but we often induce ourselves into hypnosis all the time during the day, which is considered self-hypnosis.

Milton Erickson, the premier hypnotism expert suggests that people hypnotize themselves every day. The self-induced hypnotic state is more subtle than the deep trance that is brought on through deliberate exercises and suggestions. Hypnosis is an instrument that can be used to make someone more self-conscious, self-aware, and use their resources to improve themselves. Hypnosis can be negative to the point where the subject or victim believes that the ideas they develop in their heads are their ideas as if it was reality. Once the victim is hypnotized the manipulator can lead the victim to believe in anything that they suggest. If they say that you are ugly, lazy, procrastinator, the victim will develop the belief that these thoughts are true and over time they will be owned by the victim as a thought or idea generated from themselves.

This is done through constant suggestion and reinforcement, that's how people from some religion are made to believe in what they believe in until death. Your mind is very susceptible to suggestion when your body is in a relaxed state. When your body is relaxed, you've zeroed in and the ideas are coming into your mind. Anything that the hypnotist tells you, you will follow all other logical thoughts or sense of self goes out the window and you will do anything the hypnotist suggests.

Hypnotism is a very powerful technique if used by very experienced individuals you have to be strong to withstand or identify when someone is trying to manipulate you through hypnosis.

Manipulators that use hypnotism act similarly to cult leaders, where through continuous suggestion and reinforcement they can get people to do things against their will. Through hypnosis, the followers are programmed to accept whatever the leader says, without second-guessing whether it's right or wrong.

Even when it goes against their personal belief and value. This is a cult-like process of indoctrination which involves repeating incantation which leads to a trance-like state similar to hypnosis.

In a recent article 'How Hypnosis is used in psychology,' it was discovered that hypnosis can be a form of alternative medicine, it can be used to manipulate our emotional states. It's commonly used to alter our natural state, hypnosis is so powerful it's being used in psychology as a treatment for many conditions, such as ADHD, dementia even arthritis (Cherry, Jan 2020). Many people who are aware of these techniques will use it on their unsuspecting victims.

These techniques lead to a consciousness altered state which is what cult leaders strive to achieve through chanting and meditation. All of your state of mind can be manipulated during hypnosis even your spiritual experiences can be altered through hypnosis.

The prolonged incantations and hypnotic inductions can affect one's ability to make conscious decisions.

Often the process the cults will use to induce their victim is an indirect form of hypnosis. If you are not aware of what hypnosis is or identify when it's being used, you won't be able to protect yourself from it. Cults will induce their victim in a trance which is known as the pre-hypnotic state through showering them with positive and special attention. This will make their subject more compliant to authority. During this phase, the hypnotist does not want anyone else close to their victim which may result in defiance from their subject. The further their victim is isolated from other people, the more susceptible they become to hypnosis, (Arons, 1981).

Covert Hypnosis is a strategy that most manipulators will use on their victims. This is where they try to communicate with another person's unconscious mind without them knowing. This is done through conversations and suggestions, the objective is to tap into the unconscious mind and change the victims' subconscious mind so that their target believes these thoughts are their own.

The target will then be unaware that they are being manipulated. The perpetrated will attempt to make their move when the target is relaxed or tired at that point critical thinking becomes more challenging and they are more susceptible to suggestions and subconscious manipulation.

Covert hypnosis is indirect and was popularized by Milton Erickson, he developed his theory which is called the Milton Model. Milton uses abstract language patterns which are unclear and ambiguous so that the target comes up with their interpretation they will believe to be their thoughts. Milton uses very vague languages so that the victim can make up their interpretations, this is done through inducing the target in a trance-like state.

Milton Model is similar to giving a client a frame, a skeleton concept, and having them fill in the missing areas based on their interpretation. It's based on the power of suggestion, suggestions that are vague and not intended for the subject to understand on a conscious level makes it so much more powerful on the victim. Because the victim will believe the thoughts they have are theirs.

Brainwashing

Brainwashing is also another form of mind control technique manipulators use to gain control of their victims. For brainwashing to work the subject has to be in an altered state of mind, reducing their ability to think critically. In this state ideas are suggested to the victim which are not theirs, then this will alter their attitude behaviors and personal belief.

Brainwashing is a very powerful technique that is also used by religious groups and cult leaders. This is a technique which is also more commonly used around us in our daily lives, you will see this being used through advertising, media, and news outlets it's constantly present among us.

The term 'brainwashing' was coined in the military from the Chinese Communist Party. They would brainwash their victims when they wanted to remove or cleanse their victims' mind, to remove any thought of the rising against the party. The Chinese Communist Party would use torture, food, and sleep deprivation along with suggestions to break the victim to believe what the party suggested to them. In the western world, brainwashing has come to mean pressurizing a target until they accept and believe a foreign idea.

Some people believe that how we behave and function today is as a result of brainwashing.

The first step in brainwashing is for the perpetrator to isolate the target, isolate them away from their family and friends. That way they can get full control over their influences and suggestions. When they are isolated they are more susceptible to respond to the technique. When the victim is isolated they have no room for outside influence and destruction. Once the victim is isolated, that's when they will begin their manipulation, they will first break down the victims' image of themselves and then suggest to them the ideas that they desire for them to believe. Some manipulators will do so through physical torture and some will brainwash their victim by mental coercion. They will tell the victims lies and bully the victim, taunting them, and make them doubt all the values and beliefs that they hold dear to themselves.

Television commercials and advertisements that we see daily for products that we often don't necessarily need is also considered a form of brainwashing. We also experience this through political campaigns, new diet fads, or a culture change. Just as any manipulation techniques the manipulator message will only target a specific group of people to influence a specific action or change in behavior. Advertising and commercials lead the target audience to get or purchase things they don't need through persuasion and mass psychology.

Persuasion can get people to do anything even if they have to compromise their values and personal beliefs. Once the manipulator gets to take over the mind and have mental control nothing is impossible. Persuasion leads the person to change the way they view things and themselves and conform to the beliefs and ideals of the manipulator.

Chapter 6:

Dark Persuasion

Some many methods and techniques are used every day to influence people to perform a specific action or change behavior. Dr. Robert Cialdini a professor in Psychology and Marketing at Arizona State University discovered that influence is based on six key principles, reciprocity, commitment, consistency, social proof, authority, liking, scarcity. Cialdini discovered that one of these principles were almost always in action when it comes to persuasion. Cialdini notices human basic behavior dictates that when we receive something we want to give something back as if we are paying back debts. We innately want to treat others as they treated us; it's a part of our primitive nature. This is what is considered as reciprocity, people by nature feel obligated to provide something in return because humans don't like to feel indebted to others. How manipulators use this principle is by offering something for free, you will see them doing favors to lure you in. After receiving these favours and freebies, humans will begin to develop a feeling of guilt and indebtedness to return something in exchange. If someone is trying to get something out of you, they will use this technique before they ask you for their favor, it's almost considered as an ethical bribe.

In 1974 Dr. Phillip Kunz performed an experiment, which demonstrated a better understanding of reciprocity in action. Dr. Kunz was a Sociologist at Brigham Young University, he decided to experiment to see what people would do if they were to receive a Christmas card from a stranger. Dr. Kunz randomly selected 600 names from the directory, wrote their names on the cards, and mailed them out. To his surprise, he was receiving back 12 to 15 cards per day, totaling to more than 200 cards. What happened to Kunz was the direct result of the principle of reciprocity.

The second principle in Caldini's persuasion principle is a commitment, Caldini declares that human beings have a deep need to be consistent. Psychologists consider this as 'Behavioral Consistency', this is where we default to the same decision to make the process of making decisions easy. Human beings don't like to make different decisions every time they are faced with problems. In Cialdini's research, he found that people will do anything they can to behave consistently, which also drives a feeling of positivity, even when they are wrong. Once someone has taken a stand, they feel compelled to behave consistently with their commitment. If they have taken a side in an argument or have decided to venture on a journey, all their actions will justify their decisions. Let's say they decided to become vegan for the new year, you will see them checking all their food items and clothes to be consistent with their decisions. They will feel a sense of pressure to keep the promise not only to themselves but also to the public eye. If we do not follow through with our decision, we will feel a sense of guilt especially if we are inconsistent with others. Which can result in us feeling anger, disappointment, and confusion, we are also afraid that our decision will affect our interpersonal relationship so we avoid undue stress and maintain our consistency.

What manipulators will do is get a person to commit to doing an action, fulfilling a promise, or changing a behavior. As I described in the previous paragraph because of our human nature to have consistency in our lives, whenever we commit to what is asked of us, we will likely follow through. Humans have a deep need to be seen as consistent, so instead of them risking themselves being seen as inconsistent, they will go to lengths to fulfill commitments that they have agreed to.

Another principle of persuasion is social proof, which Cialdini describes as us doing what we see other people doing because people believe that they are safer in numbers. We are more likely to behave in a way that we see as acceptable or try an activity that we see a lot of people doing. If we are passing a store and it's always filled with people, we are likely to go inside that store and shop, especially when the people we observe share some similarities with us. If we observe that a lot of people with similarities to us share an interest in something, it's by our human nature to be interested in the same thing. Cialdini found that people will conform to be liked or to be similar to everyone else and be accepted in societies. The manipulator will use this technique to show their victims how many other people that are similar to them that have performed the same actions or behave in the same way. Through this, they can win your trust and spur a desire in you to be similar to everyone else. That's how manipulators can get their victims to do whatever it is that they want of them. For example, if you work in an environment where everyone is cheating and behaving in an unethical manner, say stealing the company's property which will expose the subject and the company at risk. A master manipulator will first bring this to your attention, by telling you all your coworkers that are stealing the company's property. By showing you this they will invite you to participate in their unethical behavior, which would lead you to do one of two things. Either you will leave the company, or you will stay and participate in these practices. It's our primitive psychology that manipulators use against us to accomplish their will.

Authority is another principle that Cialdini discovered to be a significant influence in persuading others to get them to do what we want. Because we grew up respecting and fearing our parents or guardians, we developed a tendency to obey authority figures. When we meet someone with authority, a doctor, police, gym instructor, teacher we are more likely to accept what that person of authority says. People will take part in negative, unethical activity even if it goes against their personal belief, once someone in authority asks them to do it. We can see it all around us, we can see it in the culture, our purchase behavior, our values, our beliefs are all subject to influence from someone in authority. Humans are generally compliant with an authority figure if that person can make themselves seem like an authority figure. We almost reluctantly follow or agree with whatever that is their recommendation.

The evidence of this theory was illustrated in an experiment conducted by Professor Stanley Milgram, a Professor of Psychology at Yale University. In this experiment test subjects were divided into two groups: teachers and learners. The learners were given word pairs to memorize for them to recall to the teachers, the teachers were told that for each wrong answer they should punish the learners with electric shock, and with each mistake, they would increase the intensity of the shock. The research showed that most of the teachers would raise the volts to 450 volts at the direction of the lab researcher that was inside the room. Even though they knew that the volts could potentially kill or permanently damage the learner. The experiment found that regardless the teachers would still raise the intensity. At one point in the experiment, the researchers had the learners ask the teachers for more volts and the teachers did not follow through with their request instead of only the request from the lab researchers. This is what the Cialdini principle of authority represents, our sense of duty inside us, our willingness to follow instructions from authority. Milgram's experiment explains perfectly that us humans are bound by a sense of compliance to any authority figure or even perceived authority.

Cialdini principle suggests that liking also plays a factor in influencing persuasion, the more you like someone the more likely you are to say yes to that person. People are more easily persuaded by people that they like and agree with, people who are more physically attractive tend to be more persuasive among their peer groups. I am sure you have heard the story about Ms.Wise that built the Tupperware empire, through her likability and persuasiveness.

Ms.Wise in an attempt to sell some containers that she received hosted a party, a party in which she was a popular guest. She would demonstrate the durability and benefits of her Tupperware among the group of women in attendance. Her strategy worked, as her sales skyrocketed through the roof. This is demonstrative of the power of persuasion when someone is liked, they have much more influence. Especially if they are aware that they are liked in the group, they will use their influence to promote their agenda or achieve their goals through the actions of others.

When you do carefully observe Cialdini's principle, I am sure you can identify that at some point in time you have used or been a victim of one of these principles. Master manipulators that understand these techniques can weave their way into anyone's mind and manipulate their behavior at will.

Chapter 7:

NLP Programming

Neuro-Linguistic Programming for short (NLP) is a pseudoscientific approach to program one's brain for success. NLP practitioners believe that there is a link between communication, language, and behavioral patterns. In short, NLP can be used to persuade people to take on a certain behavior which can lead to them reaching a specific goal. It's a method where the manipulator uses mild hypnosis through suggestions and conversation for persuasion. For NLP to be effective the manipulator has to make strong connections with their subjects, through effective communication for the result to be strong and lasting.

The manipulator has to be persuasive and confident in their approach or the technique will not work. We are going to look at several of the techniques manipulators use to persuade their victims.

Mind Mapping

Mine mapping is an individual perception of the world, how they see things about the world. What NLP does is teaches us that our mind, body, and language are all wrapped together which give us our perception of the world or (map). You can tell the behavior of a person from the words that they use and how they interpret events in the world. The general concept of mental maps is that we live our lives based on our perception of the world, if we see the world as abundant we live as though there is an infinite supply. If our perception of the world is lacking or limiting, we live as though the world is scarce. How we see everything is filtered through our personal beliefs, experiences, and our upbringing.

Manipulators will use mental maps to try to build deeper connections, to increase their influence over you. Remember that for NLP to work effectively, there have to be strong and genuine connections. What a practitioner of NLP will do is get their subject to expand their thinking, explore other ideas, and worldview. Which would make it easier for them to understand and connect with others that have alternative views?

Modeling

Modeling is when you study someone else's behavior, language, strategies, and beliefs to copy and then create a model for yourself. People will do this to achieve the same or similar result to what the other person is getting systematically.

You will see this alot inside an organization, a candidate battling over position and promotion will model or shadow the person they aspire to be, to eventually one day operate in a similar capacity or even better. Manipulators will befriend, go covert, and study the behavior of their victims if they see it benefiting them, especially if they want what you have or want to be who you are. When someone is modeling the other person, they will suspend their ideas, beliefs, language to effectively become the one they admire. When the admirer has identified how to model behavior successfully, they can learn and teach any new skill effortlessly, which would make them even more persuasive.

Which is what is necessary for a manipulator to gain more control over their victims.

The Milton Model

This is the same Milton Erickson that we made mention of prior when we discuss hypnosis and hypnotherapy. The Milton Erickson model is embraced in NLP because of its ability to induce trance to tap deep inside the reservoir of someone's personality. The Milton Model has three aspects to induce its subject into a trance, these include rapport building, overloading conscious attention, and indirect communication.

Milton states that rapport building is used to build and strengthen greater communication flow between the two. The practitioner will pace or tune the subject to understand their mind map. Once they have accomplished that, they will then change and lead their subject to accept their perception so that the victim can follow suit. Once both are in harmony with each other, the manipulator can now get the subject to do as they desire.

The second stage is to overload the victims' conscious attention, this is done through being ambiguous in their language and communication, both verbal and nonverbal. When suggestions are vague, it distracts the conscious mind in figuring out what is meant, which leaves the unconscious mind the room to thrive and work.

The third aspect in the Milton Model is Indirect communication, this takes place during the overload of conscious attention. The communication is purposely vague to access the unconscious mind to gain influence over it. A direct suggestion would sound like, 'Why don't you go up to talk to that girl, you know you will not be nervous' ' vs an indirect suggestion "When you are speaking to the girl, you might feel even more confident in yourself". The indirect language allows the subject to fill in the finer details. The sole purpose of this is to gain access to the conscious mind, through which you can influence the person's behavior and actions.

Chapter 8:

The Everyday Sadist

The Sadist is one of many personality types that you will encounter on a day to day basis. The "Sadists derive pleasure or enjoyment from another person's pain, yet new research shows that sadist behavior ultimately deprives sadists of happiness" (Chester.D, 2018). The sadists are intrinsically motivated, meaning they are driven by internal rewards, how they will feel inside after they follow through with their actions. Sadists gain pleasure from inflicting pain and suffering on innocent people, for the cruelty and pain is pleasurable, exciting and to some, it can be sexually stimulating. Sadism, psychopathy, narcissism, Machiavellianism all have overlapping characteristics, which involve being callous, manipulative, exploitative, self-centered, and disagreeableness. The above personalities also come together to form the Dark Triad as discussed earlier.

Studies have shown that those who are high in sadism and low in empathy, were more willing to show aggression against innocent people. Sadists would increase their aggression when they realize that the person would not fight back. Sadists are willing to extend themselves and spend more time and energy going out of their way at every opportunity they have to hurt their victims. Erin Buckel, a professor at the University of British Columbia researched discovered to what extent are everyday sadists willing to go to hurt people. Everyday sadists possess an internal motivation to hurt other people, however, they are unwilling to act out if they can be criminal or dangerous, (E.Buckel, 2013). In Erin's research, she came up with laboratory tasks that mimic the harming behavior people might produce in their daily lives. She reproduces tasks that would not hurt anyone but seem to the test subject as though they are hurting someone.

Erin uses the task of killing a bug, arguing that this would satisfy the sadist desires to cause harm to a living creature. They test their theories by offering the participants the option to choose an unpleasant task of which killing bugs is one of them. They had bug-killing among three choices; cleaning dirty toilets, putting their hand in a bucket of ice. The bug-killing however wasn't real, but it was simulated to make it seem as if it was real. They found that the highly sadistic subjects were most likely to choose big killing over the other tasks. Which they reported as being pleasurable. The subject also said if they were to regret not taking on a task it would be the bug-killing tasks.

In the second experiment the highly sadists were given a task of blasting white noises in their counterparts' ears that were less cruel than them. They were first made to believe that their opponent would not attack them if they were to blast the music in their ear. There were no actual opponents, the situation was rigged, the sadists were quicker to harm their opponents and blast the music in their ear. The sadist would blast the music more at every opportunity they get, the experiment reflects good evidence to how sadists behave in a day to day environment. The sadist has the potential to kill and harm innocent opponents that have not inflicted harm on them. Unlike the other members of the dark triad that have to experience some pain to inflict pain on others. The sadists get their kicks from inflicting pain on their victims that have done nothing to them. For this reason, it makes them one of the most dangerous of all among the dark triad.

Dealing With Deception

Deception is another form of manipulation to make people believe something or information provided is not true. The most common form of deception as we all may know is lying, lying is when someone knows something to be untrue but presents the information to make it appear to be true to deceive their victim.

Everyone at some time or another engages in some form of deception, we either do it to protect ourselves, prevent ourselves from pain, or forward our cause and desires. Deception is an inevitable part of our lives, studies show that we are lied to at least 10-200 times per day, and we lie 1-2 times per day. We usually lie to avoid an uncomfortable situation or to not hurt someone's feelings. Deception is high in cultures that have low trust and high corruption, and low in societies with high sanctions against lies and corruption. Even in cases where the person is omitting or concealing information, which is considered as hiding the truth or intent to attempt to deceive the other person. Even in mere silence just by them withholding information from you indicate intentions to deceive the other. Some will go as far as fabricating a story to deceive their victim(s).

Deception also takes the form of people telling themselves lies, they may do it for self-esteem reasons or they are just delusions. For example, a person may tell themselves they can do something impossible or improbable, such as someone that's overweight and below-average height telling themselves they can make it to the NBA. Experts argue that this type of behavior may be harmful to the victim if someone insists on believing in an idea to go against all the existing facts.

Chapter 9:

Protect Yourself Against Manipulation

Before you try to learn how to protect yourself against a manipulator, you need to first know how to identify when someone is trying to manipulate you. A manipulator's influence usually comes from their ability to make you feel fear, obligation, and guilt. This is how they get you to do things that you don't want to do, through the different psychological techniques. Manipulators will often make you feel obligated or a sense of fear to do what they desire. Or some will put you in a state of guilt, once you realize that this person is constantly trying to manipulate your emotions you should get out of that relationship.

People sometimes confuse a manipulator with a bully, however, they are different while a manipulator uses aggression and threat to intimidate their victims and gain control of them. Master manipulators will act as if they are the victim, they are very good at drawing the victim card when they are the ones that caused the problem. All of their strategies are based on psychology, gaining control of their victims' minds. Their objective is to make you feel guilty and responsible for helping them, they will blame everyone but themselves for everything that goes wrong. That's one of the reasons why manipulators at times play "nice", in an attempt to gain favors from other people.

Their strongest weapon is guilt and comparison, they will compare what they did for you to what you did for them, or compare what someone else did for them versus what you did. They will use terms such as

"After all, I have done for you" or "So and so did this and that " or "this is what so and so think of you". You will hear a lot of those especially if you are inside an intimate relationship. Because of human nature, we will tend to want to reciprocate the favor that was given to us.

When you observe that you are dealing with a manipulator, one of the best ways to deal with them is to just avoid their company entirely. If you do not give them a chance to interact with you, you do not have to worry about falling or being susceptible to their manipulative behavior. The only time you should interact with a manipulator is unless you have to, such as in a situation where you are working and have to interact with them for jobs. The more you keep your distance the better off you will be.

A manipulator's main objective is to point out your faults and weaknesses to make you feel inadequate about yourself, especially when it comes to satisfying their expectations.

If you ever find yourself feeling like this, remember that you are not the problem and that you are enough. When you are in these types of relationships, you have to constantly ask yourself these questions, if what they are asking of you is reasonable, is this a one-way relationship, do you feel empowered in the relationship? This will help you come to terms with the fact that you need to terminate that relationship, these questions give you clues as to what the relationship is. When you find the truth and the answers are clear this will encourage you to avoid this person, clarity is very important when dealing with a manipulator. The clearer the better you will be at decision making. When you encounter a manipulator making unrealistic requests, you need to begin to ask them probing questions as it relates to the matter so that they see that you are figuring them out and that you are not standing for their exploitation. When you probe them they will begin to see the flaws in their request or expectations. You can Point holes in their request by asking them if "their request is reasonable", "Does this sound fair to you?", " is it that you are asking me to do this". When you ask these probing questions the manipulator will now begin to see that they have selfish ways that are seen to be evil. At this point, the manipulator will then begin to withdraw and back down from their demand. Their biggest threat is for them to be discovered. But a pathological manipulator such as a narcissist will dismiss your questions and even make you feel guilty about asking them questions, even dismissing it as audacious.

What manipulators also do is pressure their victims into making quick decisions, this will lead the victim to make irrational poorly thought out choices. They will often block you in a corner where your options are limited and pressure you to make decisions that will benefit them and their purpose. In these circumstances what you should do is find a way to buy time, use the time to your benefit, this way you can distance yourself from them and think clearly with better information.

Saying something as simple as "I'll think about it" is sufficient to buy you some more time. In this time take your time to evaluate the pros and cons of the idea and the implications of whichever decision you make. You can use the time to negotiate something in your favor or simply just say no to whatever the request may be.

If the relationship is a professional one you can say no in an articulate manner that will preserve a workable relationship. This could even be with a family member, a friend, or an acquaintance, only if you must do so. If the relationship is toxic don't be afraid to say no without giving it a second thought. Manipulators like to prey on the weak, people that are compliant, and accepting of their behavior you make yourself a target. Whenever you stand up for yourself and show some backbone they will begin to back off because they are cowards, you will observe this in the corporate environment and schoolyard. The best defense against a manipulator is to oppose them by standing up for yourself.

Chapter 10:

Psychological Warfare

(PSYWAR)

This is a form of a psychological operation to evoke action through implementing psychological techniques and methods, really its purpose is to get people to react with a certain behavior. Psychological warfare is aimed at changing the victims' value system, personal beliefs, emotions, reasonings, and behavior. It's often referred to as mass psychology. Manipulators use psychological warfare to control their victims, to think in a specific pattern, to reinforce behaviors and attitude. Psychological warfare is often used in wars against enemies, especially POWs, to destroy their morale and break down their psychological states. Even though this manipulative strategy is often used among soldiers, it's not limited to them, several target audiences for this tactic are among governments, groups, and individuals. This type of warfare is usually done through media and other communication technology that can reach a wider audience. The media is the foremost most powerful tool in psychological warfare. Psychological warfare's objective is to strip away your views and change public opinion towards an ideology. They will make you begin to doubt and question your own beliefs and actions, questioning yourself of the validity of your belief. Anyone in the world with enough resources can indulge in psychological warfare through mass communication. Especially in these times where we have the internet and people can freely spread misinformation throughout the world.

Psychological Warfare is a "War of the Mind", back in the world war, it was tactical use of threats, propaganda, and con-combative techniques that were used to influence the thinking and behavior of an enemy. Its purpose was to influence morale, you will also see it being used in highly competitive sports, such as boxing, football, rugby, hockey, and soccer. Some people refer to this as trash talk, it's meant to intimidate and win psychological warfare over their opponents, as once they are defeated mentally they can be defeated physically. When psychological warfare is well planned, the tactic is to first gain total control over the opponent's beliefs, thoughts dislikes and likes over their target. This is done through media communication, that's why the media is such a powerful tool for the elite.

It's the best way to capture the "minds and hearts" of the people, once you have the people on your side then you can do whatever you want. When you are aware of these efforts you can protect yourself against such psychological control and influence. Information can be used as a form of weaponry, to protect yourself you have to either remove yourself from it or confront it head-on. Any tool that can or have been used to disseminate information can be used in psychological warfare. These may come in the form of audiovisual, movies, radio, newspapers, books, magazines, or posters. This is one of the main reasons why during a political campaign, it's the party that has the most money and resources that wins the election. Because of the power of influence through communication.

Psychological warfare is also very prevalent in the workspace, people are in constant competition, fighting for promotion and opportunities constantly. Psychological warfare in the workplace takes the form of suggestion, bickering, and gossip, he says. Once the victim falls for it, they can be outmaneuvered and thrown off course or out of your position. They will use these tactics to close in on promotions, they will say they will help you and not deliver on it, all in that time they are working on overtaking you. To protect yourself against these techniques you first need to know how to identify them and how to use them to your benefit. Having suggestions can help you influence the way you act and react in a given situation. Once you suggest to yourself that an expected outcome will occur if you take a specific action, the more likely it is to occur. This is because of the thoughts you entertain accompanied by behavior. For example, if you believe that visiting a client in a better-looking car will give you a certain amount of respect which would make the deal go in your favor, then more than likely you will act as if which will positively impact the outcome of the deal in your favor.

This tactic of suggestion can make you or break you. Just by suggesting the negative if you don't count those negative suggestions with positive, this will influence the outcome of your behavior and hence the results. Psychological scientist Maryanne Garry and Robert Michael published an article Current Directions in Psychological Science. The study explored the relationship between, suggestion, cognition, and behavior. What they discovered is that suggestion can influence a person's performance, even when it comes to medicine, which is known as the placebo effect. The power that suggestion has on our lives is what we call 'response expectancies', this is where we automate our response in an anticipated situation which creates the outcome.

Once we anticipate a specific outcome, every action will ensure that the outcome comes to fruition. If a shy person believes that when they go out with their friends they will be more confident, when they go out with friends, they will feel, less inhabited and approach more people and be more friendly. The article has concluded that we have significant power over many of our outcomes, by simple suggestion and expectancies. Deliberate suggestions influence expectations that influence behavior.

So when you are interacting with people and they suggest things to you, which has a negative outcome, what you need to do is counter that by being positive and expecting good results. Several studies have even shown that suggestions can make a person more successful. Suggestions can have both a negative and positive effect on an individual. This is the greatest defense you have against psychological warfare, remove your exposure to negativity, or once you are exposed to any negative suggestion counter it with positivity. There is a war for your mind, and for the control of your mind, it's always happening from an individual level, group level to a government level. Your only defense you have is you.

See Through Their "Masking"

A facade (pronounced "sad") is a front that people put up emotionally, they could be mad and upset but you will see them smiling. They will put up a facade to hide how they truly feel about a situation. It's not just from a victim standpoint, but manipulators will also show a face to not let you know their true intentions, that's how they gain leverage over their victims. People will put on a facade because of fear, fear of being found out, fear of being victimized, fear of being seen as weak. Especially when we are insecure, insecurities are seen as weaknesses hence most people tend to hide their insecurities. Some people might be insecure about their jobs, about their finances, about their spouses, about their weight.

Often you will tend to see people smile or laugh when the conversation gets uncomfortable, this is the facade they put on to hide that they might be offended or insecure about what was said. Bullies can hide behind the mask of anger, we hide behind the mask of our finances by buying more stuff we can't afford just to prove to people that we can afford it. We put on a mask that we are happily married when our marriage is in shambles to save face.

A facade is also referred to as personality masking, we do this to conform to social and peer pressure, to be accepted, and to blend in. Masking is often developed during our childhood years when we are around our parents. We show one face different from that we show our friends and a lot of people refer to this as being sneaky or two-faced. It's simple measures we take to protect ourselves and prevent other people from being hurt or knowing the uncomfortable truth. Many of your coworkers, friends, family, and spouses are doing this, you have to be analytical and observant to identify when they are masking/facade or when they are not. Many people put on a personality facade to prevent themselves from being judged by others, hurt, and attacked by other people. You will find that a lot of people that live alternative lifestyles also put on a facade to blend in. Because they do not want to have to deal with the challenges that come with them showing their real selves. When people put on a facade they are role-playing, as if they are following a script with an end or outcome in mind. Facades can be in the form of showing material items we own, bragging about careers, about assets, about places we've visited. It's oftentimes used to hide something deeply embedded inside. Especially when manipulators are trying to gain our trust, they will try their best to fit in this role for you to accept and believe them before they begin to subtly gain an advantage over your mind and emotions. But putting on a facade allows us to appeal to others and gain their friendship, to have our needs met by those whose attention we seek. When our mask is on we feel more confident about ourselves around those that we admire or those that we are trying to win their trust.

Chapter 11:

Psychological Mind Games

Psychological mind games come when the other party tries to have one-upmanship against the others through passive-aggressive behavior. The objective is to disempower you mentally to gain superiority over the subject. Everyone at some point or another employs or plays mind games, however the manipulator masters the art of mental manipulation and having power over their victim through gaining power over their mind. It's a struggle for superiority, favor, and prestige, it appears every day in the corporate world, sports, relationships, and especially politics.

In an office environment, it's hard to see as people do try their best to be politically correct and not sabotage working relationships. We all have to prepare to meet a variety of mind games from our rivals attempting to gain an edge over us mentally. It's a constant battle and the more we are aware of it the easier it is for us to combat it and win.

Mind games will come in the form of suggestions, social undermining, and downplaying. Social undermining often occurs in the workplace, where negative emotions are often directed to someone as a way of preventing the person from achieving their goals. The behavior is used to hinder the target from accomplishing whatever their goal is. Social undermining can affect a person's mental health, which can even cause depression. People use social undermining to make the other person look bad, slow, and incompetent. They will even go as far as to ruin your reputation, to make you look small. Undermining can make a person doubt themselves and question their competence, belief, and perception. That's why it's very important to be self-assured when you are being undermined by someone else.

Minimization of downplaying is another form of mind game that people play to gain an advantage or control over your mind. Minimization is the opposite of exaggeration, the term is self-explanatory, this is where someone downplays the significance of an emotion or an event that occurred. Manipulators often use this when they are being confronted with guilt, to hide their true intent. Manipulators will downplay any misdemeanors when confronted, if they notice positive attributes within the person they will also downplay their skills and talents. The main purpose of this technique is to downplay the ills of their actions and downplay any positive attributes of their victim to make them think less of themselves.

The more you can defeat your victim mentally the more control you can have of their actions. Manipulators will downplay their actions to seem altruistic, to make it appear that it's for the common good for everyone.

Gaslighting is quite similar to minimization, it's another form of psychological mind games. Where the manipulator sows seeds and thoughts in the mind of their victim to make them question their perception, ideals, and judgment. They aim to make the victim doubtful of themselves by using contradiction, denial, misinformation, and misdirection. The victim's beliefs are delegitimize, which in turn affects their self-confidence and self-esteem. Once the victim has become more vulnerable, that's when the manipulator will then swoop in and disorientate the victim and control their minds.

The term gaslighting originated from a 1940 stage play, where a husband manipulates his wife by changing small elements around her environment. After she begins to question what she sees, he manages to convince her that she is insane, mistaken, or going delusional. The husband slowly dims the gaslight in their home, while pretending that nothing has changed to make his wife doubt her perception. The wife constantly asks her husband about the subtle changes, but he keeps insisting that she is going insane. Once the manipulator effectively gets the person to doubt their perception that's when they will begin to coerce their victim to get them to do what they want them to do. The manipulator convinces the victim that their ideas and perceptions are false and that the victimizer's ideas are correct.

Then makes the victim question their thinking and adopt the belief that they have disturbing ideas, which result in the feeling of helplessness. When they are in this state they are more susceptible to the control and power of the manipulator.

When you do think about it your mind is the most powerful thing that you have in your possession, your mind can make or break you. We must always take guard and control over our faculties.

Operant Conditioning

Positive Reinforcement

Positive reinforcement is the reinforcement of a specific behavior through rewarding, you may at times hear the term comes from a theory known as operant conditioning. This is used to promote the recurrence of behavior in the future, the reward is given to the subject after the favorable outcome, this helps to strengthen the behavior in the future. For example, if a person asks you to act, say wash up plates, every time you wash the plates they give you a slice of cake. That's positive reinforcement, it's meant to reinforce a specific behavior. So with a manipulator, once they get you to do what they wish, they will reward you to reinforce the behavior. Positive reinforcement happens daily in random situations, you may hold the door for a person and they smile at you and say thanks, that makes you feel good inside and reinforces that behavior. You will find yourself performing the behavior again in the future. However in most cases, positive reinforcement is deliberate, it's used to train and effect power and maintain a specific behavior. You will see a lot of dog lovers use this technique to get their dogs to perform an action or maintain a discipline. You will see them commanding their dogs to sit, or roll over and then giving them a treat right afterward.

Once someone can control your actions, or attempt to control your actions, you are being manipulated. Not all manipulations are bad, some are meant for good. For instance, when you perform at work, by meeting your KPI or your monthly quota, you are rewarded with a commission, recognition, bonuses, and kudos from the boss. This is one technique that is practiced in our society daily because of the result that it yields. Have you ever wondered why, or how someone from a good home can be coerced into becoming a serial killer or, savage? One of the reasons and tactic use is positive reinforcement when their victim performs their malicious deeds, their behaviors are reinforced by the victimizer in different ways. It's the same as if a parent would get a child to steal for them and reinforce their behaviors by giving them candy or make them play with toys. Once you are aware of this, if someone is trying to manipulate you through positive reinforcement you can simply decline the reward to further prevent yourself from being controlled.

Negative Reinforcement

Negative reinforcement is also a part of the B.F Skinner operant conditioning theory. With negative reinforcement, the behavior is reinforced by removing an unpleasant or negative outcome. This form of manipulation is when the victim is placed in uncomfortable circumstances or discomfort, which could be physical, economical, and psychological. The negative reinforcement is removed when the desired behavior is performed. The manipulator will allow the victim to escape the negative stimuli that are present when they do what is expected of them.

Negative reinforcement is the removal/avoidance of pain, such as doing your homework to avoid getting low grades. There is a fine line between negative reinforcement and punishment, which are often misconstrued. Punishment is the addition of a negative stimulus to change undesired behavior. An example of this is when you are grounded after you receive low grades at school, or get into a fight. Once something is being added as a consequence of a behavior, that's punishment and once something is being removed as a consequence of a behavior that's negatively reinforced.

Chapter 12:

Toxic Environments

A Lot of times the relationship we have with a person or the environment that we are in is toxic. The earlier we can identify toxic relationships the faster we can remove ourselves from that situation. A lot of toxic people have had open emotional scars from their past that they carry around. And what they do is in turn transfer this emotional hurt and baggage to someone else. Which often takes the form of victimizing people, bullying, and manipulation.

Toxic people go around and create drama and issues in other people's lives, they think all about themselves and use others to fulfill their needs. Their toxic behaviors come in the form of jealousy, manipulation, narcissistic behavior, enviousness, and begrudging. These behaviors make the victim feel sad, betrayed, withdrawn, and at times even lonely. You may even find yourself becoming dependent on them instead of relying on your own opinion. When you interact with toxic people they will make you feel emotionally drained to the point where you just give up whatever it is that you were going after.

You will know when you are dealing with a toxic person as you become more anxious, pessimistic, and apprehensive about every situation. These people become very judgemental about you during the development of the relationship and they refuse to take responsibility for their actions, they have no level of accountability. So you will find that their lives are often out of control physically and financially as well and if you allow them to infiltrate your life, your life will in turn become similar. They do not want to own up to their shortcoming, they want you to feel sorry for them and fix their problems. When they play the victim role and get you to sympathize with them, that's when they use your emotions against you and get you to do things you would not normally do. Then you get into a cycle which never ends, because there is always an issue with them, they will even create problems for others to empathize with them, as misery loves company. Every minute you spend around them is unfulfilling because all of your emotions are focused on taking care of the issues that they have.

Once you detect or notice that you are in a toxic relationship you can either confront them about this and ask them to change or leave the relationship. Because if you maintain this type of toxic relationship it will only result in negative consequences for yourself. The toxic person's main purpose is to gain influence and control over other people, they are demanding and will make you feel guilty when you are not able to meet their expectations. They will want your undivided attention, they will even go to the point of isolating you from your other friends and family members. It may be very hard to leave these types of situations but it makes no sense being involved with someone that seeks to control you, drain you, and makes you feel bad about yourself. Always put yourself first no matter the circumstances.

Final Chapter:

Owning Your Dark Side

All of us have a dark side and it tends to come out either at our worst moments or when it's most necessary, such as to protect ourselves and reputation. We don't often reveal these types of traits to people, it's something we're not too proud of, it's behaviors that we are ashamed of and are embarrassed about. And if you look inside yourself you should be able to identify these traits if you are truly honest with yourself.

For myself, I tend to be a little bit manipulative when I want something out of my friends, at times I might be selfish as well. I will always give to my friends because I know that down the road they can reciprocate the favor, one hand washes the other. At times that may come off as a little bit manipulative, but it's something we all do whether we are aware of it or not.

Other people might fight their Darkside being that they are judgemental, lazy, selfish, toxic, or even controlling. Once you find your Darkside, be wary of it, and instead of making it work against you inside your relationship, make it work for you and to the benefit of others. If it's toxic behavior, eliminate it, but a lot of times our insecurities and dark behaviors push us to become better. It may push you to prove yourself good in the eyes of others by doing charitable works. We might seek therapy and hence become mentors to other people, we may even start a project and initiative that can change the world. Like an ex-drug addict starting social projects to help children say no to drugs, or an ex bull teaching students why bullying is wrong or even how to stand up to a bully. What's important is that we embrace our Darkside and make it work for us instead of against us.

Our Darkside has our innate primitive behaviors and pleasures, it's the side that we are afraid to show other people. That's one of the reasons why I said everyone puts up a facade at some point or another. Some of us wish that our dark sides would go away, however, but they won't and nothing is wrong with that. What we need to do is try to turn lemons into lemonade or suppress our feelings to the point where it's not toxic to other people. We must learn to accept ourselves rather than judge, when we become more accepting of who we are we begin to face reality and discover ways to manage our behaviors.

If you can take time to list and recognize all of your manipulative and dark side behavior, you can reflect on them and figure out how you can use them to help yourself. How you can use them to your advantage to better your life and the lives of others around you. You should try and monitor yourself to see when they are triggered and how you respond. When you become more sensitive towards yourself you will now have more clarity as to what to do in future situations or how it is that you will correct the dark side and use it to your benefit. On the other hand, ensure that you are aware and take notice of the dark side of others. To protect yourself against malicious and manipulative actions, the more you take notice of yourself and others the better.

I wish you Best of Luck, please feel free to leave an honest review on this book, please.

THE END

9 798674 829539